A Horse Racing System Based On A Statistical Approach To Selection And Staking

Lucky Lew

Copyright © 2012 Lucky Lew

All rights reserved.

ISBN-13: 978-1490940939

DEDICATION

This book is dedicated to all of those people out there who struggle to make a profit on horse racing.

ACKNOWLEDGMENTS

I would like to acknowledge all of the punters online who contribute to forums, discussions and communities. Without you there would be no new ideas and concepts on which this horse racing system was developed.

The Photo for the cover was provided by FreeDigitalPhotos.net.
The original owner of the image is user ponsulak. This image has been used under the free digital photo rights as stated by the terms and conditions on FreeDigitalPhotos.net

INTRODUCTION

Horse Racing systems are notorious for working for short periods of time or over historical data but they always seem to start to fall over when you start to place money on the selections. This is usually because of back fitted results and the systems producer having no background in statistics and probability. It has also been identified that horse racing punters are quick to pick up on anomalies which slowly erode the odds and value. The system explained in this book is very different to the selection processes of most systems as it takes into account statistical analysis and horse racing truths and makes money from them.

This Horse Racing System is consistent, easy to follow and profitable. It is all of these things because the rules for it are not subjective and are all based on statistical analysis. It also uses at its heart principles and statistics which have been known to all horse racing punters, but it uses them to profit.

So what are these horse racing truths that we can take advantage of?

Well there are several and they include:

- Favourites win 30% of the time
- The odds market is the best guide to a horses chance in a race
- Favourites win more races earlier in the card and their strike rate drops as the card progresses
- There is a favourite / long shot bias in the way most mug punters place bets.
- The Law of averages
- The psychology of the punter and their ability to go on "tilt" as it's called in poker.

FAVOURITES WIN 30% OF THE TIME

It is a well known statistic that favourites win on average approx 29%-32% in thoroughbred racing. This average is slightly higher in harness (trots) racing and slightly lower in greyhound racing. This statistic has been shown over years and years of research.

It can move around from week to week and month to month and even year to year but overall the results always revert to an average somewhere around the 30% mark. The exact figure will depend on the data set you are analyzing

This is an important statistic in horse racing. It shows you that overall the punting effectiveness of the gambling public is still only right approximately 30% of the time.

THE ODDS MARKET IS THE BEST GUIDE TO A HORSES CHANCE IN A RACE

It has been proven through extensive research that crowds as a whole are much better at predicting the probability of something happening then individual experts. This same phenomenon also exists in horse racing and the results are clear to see in the odds market. It is well known that the favourite wins more races then the second favourite, and the second favourite wins more races then the third favourite, etc. Also when you take out the commission or tax from the odds market the odds generally will lead to a perfect fit of the horses chances over time.

For example if a horse starts at $3.00 in decimal odds (after tax and commission have been removed) then its chances of winning a race is 33%. This doesn't mean it will win the race, it just means that over 100 races it should win close to 33 races. Even 100 races is not enough to even out the statistical variation though so it may need 1000 races or more. But if we looked at 10,000 races of horses starting at $3.00 we should see approximately 3333 races won.

So if we know this information and know that the crowd is probably more informed then us and they can make a much closer prediction to the horses real chances then we can, how are we going to beat them? The answer will come soon but something to think about is why compete with the best guide to a horse's chances when instead you can use this information to your advantage.

FAVOURITES WIN MORE RACES EARLY IN THE CARD AND THE STRIKE RATE DROPS AS THE CARD PROGRESSES

Favourites tend to have a much higher strike rate in the earlier races on a card then the later races. This occurs for several reasons. The first is that the first few races are generally the lower class races and there is a wider gap in the abilities of the horses. As the card progresses the better type races are run including Group races where there is a far less gap in the ability of the horses. For example in a maiden race there may only be a couple of horses who really have a chance of winning a race in their lifetime. The other horses will never win a race. Compare this to a Group 1 race where all the horses have tremendous ability and all of them have won races against other good horses as they progressed through the classes.

The second reason for this is that when most people start to do the form they start with Race 1 then progress to Race 2, etc. This means that they analyse the earlier races on the card when their mind is fresh. As they progress through the card they get tired, bored and inundated with information overload. This is leads to much better and thorough analysis on the earlier races compared to the last race.

Using this information it should be clear that the market is actually going to be a much better guide in the earlier races compared to the later races in a card. This is something we can take advantage of over a long time frame.

THERE IS A FAVOURITE AND LONG SHOT BIAS IN MOST MARKETS

University professors and doctorate students have done extensive research into the favourite/ long shot bias which exists in most markets. They have found that Betfair has done a lot to reduce this bias but that it still exists in some markets and that it particularly still exists at the lower odds.

The basic premise behind this bias is that punters will overestimate the chances of a long shot and thus they will over bet it making it little value, and the reverse is also true in that they will underestimate the chances of a horse and it will be under bet.

The shorter the odds (and greater the chance of winning) the more likely there is value for the punter. For example if the NBA All Stars team was to take on the New Zealand basketball team in a match you would expect the NBA All Stars to win 10000 matches out of 10000 matches. They would win 100% of the time, but generally the odds on offer may still exist whether that be by backing the NBA All Stars or by laying the NZ team. Any odds would be value as it's practically a no lose situation

THE LAW OF AVERAGES

The law of averages states that while the short term strike rate of an outcome may deviate significantly from the average, the longer term strike rate will always move towards the true average. How this applies to us is that we know the average strike rate of favourites is around 30%. But in a short term such as a card the average may be higher or lower than the 30%.

Favourites might only win 20% today but win 40% tomorrow to hold the average at 30%. If we know the average will help us long term then we just need to weather the storm in the shorter term.

Many people attempt to use this long term average verse short term average discrepancy with forms of a martingale system. Martingale systems are those that increase your bet after a loss to recover your stake and a small profit. There is nothing wrong with this until you get a lot of losers in a row. Still martingale staking has its place in any good money management staking system to produce optimal profits in the short term. But it needs a number of checks to ensure it doesn't get out of control and destroy your punting bank.

THE PSYCHOLOGY OF THE PUNTER

Most punters do not have the ability to profit from gambling whether it be on sports or horse racing.

They cannot handle the inevitable losses which occur. A losing run to the average punter is a reason to throw away the current system and move onto the next system in the hope it will be better. I know this from first hand experience and it is hard to withstand a losing run regardless of how much profit it has shown in the past. The reason being is we are waiting for things to change and no longer work and the latest losing run confirms it.

The psychology of the punter requires a constant winning streak with very few losing runs. The punter is going to need to feel comfortable with any system if it is to work long term.

This system ensures that no long losing runs are experienced and thus aids the punter in keeping the system going for extended periods.

Consistency is the key to any winning system for the average punter.

HOW THIS SYSTEM IS DIFFERENT AND EXPLOITS THE MYTHS AND IDEAS ALREADY DISCUSSED

You now know the reasons why systems fail if you have been reading everything up to this point. You also know a few of the undeniable truths of punting and horse racing.

This system attempts to use these truths and ideas in order to provide you with a long term system which will stand the test of time and continue to give you profits for years to come.

It does this by:

- Taking advantage of the consistently high strike rates of favourites

- Using the crowd as a filter to find the most consistent winners

- Places bets on the best races of the day to ensure consistent winners

- Understands and takes advantage of the bias in the punters betting

- Taking advantage of averages and consistency that are a keys to winning

- Caters the punters psychology to help them win consistently long term

It should be noted the above stresses consistency. Consistency is the key to long term profits..

THE BASIC THEORIES HOL;DING UP OUR SYSTEMATIC APPROACH

There are some very key elements to how this system works. Its all based to take advantage of the long term truths which were described in the first section. The basic elements of the system include:

- Only take highly consistent winning bets on Favourites

- Minimize your outlay on selections

- Implement a gradual martingale system with stop points

- Assess your Risk before betting

- Stop When you are in Profit

- Look at the profit on a day by day verse a bet by bet basis

- Have an adequate betting bank

- Spread your risk across multiple race cards

These elements are fundamental to the way the system works. It would do you very little good in your overall punting life if I just gave you rules without giving you a full understanding of why the rules exist.

RULE 1: TAKE HIGHLY CONSISTENT WINNING BETS

The horse's which are the most consistent winners are favourites.

Overall though if you had backed every favourite you would lose over the long term because the odds for winners are not high enough to overcome the losing bets.

But favourites are still the most undervalued selection due to the favourite / long shot bias and they are the most likely horse to win as the crowd is the best estimator of a horse's chances.

As we know they win at approximately 3 out of every 10 races and they are more likely to win in the early races compared to the later races on a card.

All of these truths point to the most consistent winners coming from favourites running early in the first few races of the meeting.

So our first rule for the system is:

**Back Favourites only and in Early Races
(Only in Races 1 through to 4).**

RULE 2: MINIMISE YOUR OUTLAY ON SELECTIONS

You want to ensure that you maximize your return for any winning selection while also minimizing your loss on any losing selections. This is done in a few steps as follows:

1. Bet more on horses the crowd has higher confidence in
2. Have your largest bets on your winners (discussed in Element 3)

The first point is pretty basic.

A horse estimated by the crowd at odds of $2.00 has roughly a 50% chance (assuming you have adjusted for taxes and commission) whereas a horse with odds of $4.00 has only a 25% chance of winning. If we understand that the crowd is the best predictor of a horses chances then we have to assume that the odds are the best guide to the horses real chances of winning.

For this reason you want to have a higher stake on the $2.00 chance compared to the $4.00 chance. This goes against some punters fundamental thoughts in that the $4.00 chance looks like more value because we win more if it runs first. The problem is that the $4.00 chance is going to lose a lot more races then the $2.00 chance.

To minimize our outlay on the favourites with longer odds we implement a "Bet To Win" type of staking. Others all call it the "Bet To Profit" or "Target Profit" staking.

Essentially this is done by deciding an amount you want to win on each selection. Let's assume for simplicity this is $10. If the horse had odds of $2.00 we would need to bet $10 on it in order to have a profit of $10. This is done by taking the profit required and dividing it by the odds minus 1.

Below is the calculation for a $2.00 chance:

Amount to Bet = Profit wanted / (Odds – 1)

Amount To Bet = $10 / (**$2.00** – 1)

Amount To Bet = $10 / 1

Amount to Bet = $10

Another worked example is below for a $4.00 horse:

Amount to Bet = Profit wanted / (Odds – 1)

Amount To Bet = $10 / (**$4.00** – 1)

Amount To Bet = $10 / 3

Amount to Bet = $3.33

You can also work this backwards to make sure you got it right.

For instance if we bet $3.33 on the $4.00 chance we would expect to receive back $3.33*$4.00= 13.32. From this you need to take you bet amount which was $3.33 and you get a profit of $9.99 which is very close to our $10 profit.

So the second rule in our system is to:

Adjust the stake amount based on the odds chances and the profit using:

Amount Bet = Profit/(odds-1)

RULE 3: MINIMISE YOUR OUTLAY ON SELECTIONS

Its well known that there is a law of averages and that any deviation in the short term from the average will eventually return to the average.

In horse racing this means that there might be a losing run of favourites for an extended period but for this run there will be a series of winners.

But do keep in mind the short term deviations can turn out longer then you think. As we have done throughout this book we will assume the favourite strike rate is 30%. That means:

- There is a 70% chance of a horse losing
- There is a 49% chance of two favourites losing in a row
- There is a 34% chance of three favourites losing in a row
- There is a 24% chance of four favourites losing in a row
- There is a 17% chance of five favourites losing in a row
- There is a 12% chance of six favourites losing in a row
- There is a 8% chance of seven favourites losing in a row
- There is a 6% chance of eight favourites losing in a row
- There is a 4% chance of nine favourites losing in a row
- There is a 3% chance of ten favourites losing in a row

I'll leave it at 10 favourites losing in a row. For this reason a pure martingale system will eventually destroy your bank when it hits the really long losing sequences. The really long losing sequence isn't where most martingale systems fail though because they usually try and recover over several wins instead.

In this case its the combination of medium losing sequences (5-8 loses) followed by more medium losing sequences (5-8 losses) which cause the trouble and the inevitable lose of a bank.

When looking at a martingale type of betting there are a few things to be wary of and understand. The first of these is the amount required to bet vs the odds.

Martingale systems aim to return a profit after a win. If you had lost 2 selections and your next bet was on a $4 chance with the aim to profit by $1 then you would just need to bet $1 to make the profit. The sequence would be

Loss of $1

Loss of $1

Bet amount $1 = Gain of $4

In this instance the outlay is $3 and the return is $4. But if your next favourite was only $1.50 you would need to bet $6.00. These bets would follow the sequence of

Loss of $1

Loss of $1

Bet amount $6 = Gain of $9

In this instance the outlay is $8 and the return is $9.

It should be obvious that the lower odds cause a much greater increase in your staking requirements and this can be a major flaw in martingale systems. For this reason anything less than $1.90 should not be bet.

With a martingale system you want to ensure that you wipe out all loses from your sequence in your next bet.

To do this you add the loss amount to your profit target. In the above example if our profit target was $1 and we lost our first bet (assume it was a $2.00 chance which means a $1 bet) then our profit target for the second bet would be $2 (which is $1 profit + $1 current loss in sequence). To reach our profit of $2 as the next bet in the sequence you will need to bet 50c (for example betting on a $5 favourite) and it loses then you would need to have a target of $2.50 in your next bet.

This leaves us with two new rules for our system:

1. **Do not bet on anything less than $1.90**

2. **Increase your profit target by your current loss each race.**

The only other problem with a martingale is that it can get out of control with very quickly and for this reason you should always have a loss point where you decide to scrape the sequence.

RULE 4: ASSESS YOUR RISK BEFORE BETTING

When you go into any investment you need to understand your worst case scenario.

Knowing your first case scenario you can assess if you are up for the risk and could handle it. This can be done on several levels for this system. It can be done for a betting bank.

How much do you need if you had a really bad run? It could also be done on a sequence of the martingale staking.

How much will you lose if you go to X races today and all are losing bets?

Firstly the decision needs to be made on how long your martingale sequence will be. This table appeared earlier but it is an interesting one which may help decide on how far to go

- There is a 70% chance of a horse losing
- There is a 49% chance of two favourites losing in a row
- There is a 34% chance of three favourites losing in a row
- There is a 24% chance of four favourites losing in a row
- There is a 17% chance of five favourites losing in a row
- There is a 12% chance of six favourites losing in a row
- There is a 8% chance of seven favourites losing in a row
- There is a 6% chance of eight favourites losing in a row
- There is a 4% chance of nine favourites losing in a row
- There is a 3% chance of ten favourites losing in a row

From this table you can determine what level you are comfortable with.

As the number of losers you are willing to accept increases so does the amount that can be lost in one sequence. I suggest at a minimum you want to stick to 5 races which means you will win 4 out of every 5 days (83% winning strike rate). I would suggest only going up to 7 though as after this point the betting amounts can start to increase dramatically. At 7 losers you still have a 92% chance of winning which is phenomenal and you will only lose 1 day out of every 10 betting.

These ranges are specifically picked to reduce the amount you need to wager with the martingale system and to also increase the consistency of winning.

So these guidelines lead us to our next rule:

Decide on 5,6 or 7 races as your stop point for the martingale staking.

Once you have picked a race point stick with it for at least a few weeks. Each price point will affect your psychology differently and I would suggest getting comfortable with less races before increasing the races to 7.

Some days there are a lot of short priced horses racing in the $1.85 - $2.00 range and this can be a concern for your risk level. If each horse started at $2.00 and you had chosen 5 races as your limit with a profit target of $1 you would be up for $1 on the first bet, $2 on the second bet, $4 on the next bet, $8 on the next bet and the final bet would be $16. This could result in a total loss of $31 units for a day. On the other hand if all favourites started at around $3.00 you would need to bet $0.50 for the first bet, $$1 for the second bet, $1.50 for the next bet, $2.25 for the next bet and $3.38 for the last bet which would only be a loss of $9.13 units.

If you work out the actual risk for your set of races you will be able to determine if the risk of the day is worthwhile. While short priced horses are more likely to get up ($2.00) more often when they do lose they can have a major impact on your staking levels.

An acceptable risk for me would be dependent on how much you are willing to risk. I would suggest the following levels for each set of races:

- 5 Races – Risk 10 units (average odds of $2.90)
- 6 Races – Risk 15 units (average odds of $2.90)
- 7 Races – Risk 25 units (Average odds of $2.90)

These risk levels were determined from experience. If a day shows odds which are greater then the risk level for that set of races then you should not bet. More than likely you will miss a winning day but the potential loss is too great to take the risk.

This adds another rule to the system

Stay within the risk parameters of the system which is 10 units for 5 races, 15 units for 6 races and 25 units for 7 races..

RULE 5: STOP WHEN YOU ARE IN PROFIT

A very crucial step of this system is to stop when you are in profit. I would even say this is the most important step of the whole system when combined with the martingale staking plan.

The punters psychology is the most important part of a successful betting system. Many systems fail to handle this and that is why a lot of them fail the punter even though they may be successful long term.

The punters mind is a very fragile asset.

To ensure a winning mind set and to be comfortable with a system a punter needs to be winning consistently. When you stop at a winner each day you have ensured that you finished the day in profit.

Some people will argue that if you have an edge then you should bet on all selections possible, and this is quite true. But our edge is a combination of betting on favourites in early races of the day using a carefully planned martingale system. We lose our edge as the day goes on and as we push the risk level on the martingale system. For this reason you should always stop when you are in profit for the day.

Another reason we do not need to bet all day long is that we have set a profit target for our martingale system and this should be what we are happy to make each day.

When you first start this target will be small but that needs to be done to ensure you are comfortable with the system and can establish a history of it winning by you. Over time you can increase the target as your bank increases and eventually you will be making a large profit almost every day.

So the next rule to our system is

Stop when you are in profit for the day

RULE 6: ASSESS YOUR PROFIT ON A DAY BY DAY VERSE BET BY BET BASIS

This is another important element of this system that tricks the psychology of the punter into a winning behaviour.

If a punter was to analyse this system on a bet by bet basis they would be back to seeing it having losing runs and a lot more losing bets then winning bets.

But if you keep a running tally in a spreadsheet that shows your profit by day instead of bet you will reinforce the positives of the system and be able to handle the occasional losing day. This is because 8-9 days out of every 10 will be winning days.

The biggest problem with most systems is they do not cater to the punters need for winning. Using this method of assessing the results on a daily basis will help to ensure you do not stop the system at a point where you may quickly recover your current losing sequence.

RULE 7: HAVE AN ADEQUATE BETTING BANK

Whenever a martingale system is used for staking a large enough bank needs to be ensured before starting. You cannot decide on your profit target for each day until you understand how much you have in your betting bank.

Firstly work out your betting bank and hopefully have it deposited in a betting account. I'll assume a betting bank of $300 for the examples below.

The next step is to divide this by 2. This ensures that if you get a losing run which has the potential to wipe out your betting bank you still have at least one more bank to recover. This leaves you with a betting bank for the system of $150.

To work out your target is very simple. You take the risk level of each day as defined in Element 4 (which was 10 units for 5 races, 15 units for 6 races and 25 units for 7 races) and divide your $150 by the risk * 10. So for 5 races we would be able to have a profit target of $150/(10*10) = $1.50 units a day.

That's not a large target I agree but the betting bank is also only $300. This means we could have 10 losing days in a row before we lost our losing bank which is very unlikely considering we will win 8 or 9 out of every 10 races.

I prefer to take a very conservative staking method but others may not agree. I would prefer to still be betting at the end of 12 months rather than going out earlier because I staked too much and became too greedy.

I warn you now that this staking is the level required. If you want to aim for a higher profit target with less money then you will likely fail and the system will be a failure. If that is the case I encourage you not to even attempt it as you are risking too much.

This leaves us with our next rule:

Bank size needs to be at least 2*(Risk Level * 10)

- For 5 races this is 200 times your target
- For 6 races this is 300 times your target
- For 7 races this is 500 times your target

RULE 8: SPREAD YOUR RISK ACROSS MULITPLE BANKS

There are sometimes tracks and meetings where favourites just fail to perform. This could be due to the track condition, the wind, the jockeys or just that the punters got it completely wrong. For this reason you do not want your races to all be at the same track. I recommend the following rules for your races:

- For 5 races have no more than 3 races on the same track
- For 6 races have no more than 3 races on the same track
- For 7 races have no more than 4 races on the same track

Using these guidelines it should be obvious that you need at least 2 meetings that are running in synch with each other, and preferably 3 meetings. You want to spread your risk across the tracks to ensure that you are not disadvantaged by a bad day at one track.

You will need to be careful in this instance because some races may have horses which start at less than $1.85 and we do not want to bet on those races. So make sure you check which races will be included and which will be excluded.

So this leaves us with our last rule:

Ensure your races are spread over at least 2 meetings and preferably more.

- **For 5 races have no more than 3 races on the same track**
- **For 6 races have no more than 3 races on the same track**
- **For 7 races have no more than 4 races on the same track**

A REVIEW OF THE RULES

The last chapter explained the underlying reasons for each of the rules so this chapter is a simple review of those rules so they are all in one place for easy reference.

- Back Favourites only and in Early Races (Races 1 through to 4).

- Do not bet on anything less than $1.90

- Adjust the stake amount based on the odds chances and the profit using

    - Amount Bet = Profit/(odds-1)

- Increase your profit target by your current loss each race.

- Decide on 5,6 or 7 races as your stop point for the martingale staking.

- Stay within the risk parameters of the system as shown below

    - 5 Races – Risk 10 units (average odds of $2.90)
    - 6 Races – Risk 15 units (average odds of $2.90)
    - 7 Races – Risk 25 units (Average odds of $2.90)

- Stop when you are in profit for the day

- Bank size needs to be at least 2*(Risk Level * 10)

    - For 5 races this is 200 times your target
    - For 6 races this is 300 times your target
    - For 7 races this is 500 times your target

- Ensure your races are spread over at least 2 meetings and preferably more.

    - For 5 races have no more than 3 races on the same track
    - For 6 races have no more than 3 races on the same track
    - For 7 races have no more than 4 races on the same track

Here is a simple decision flow to determine if you are ready to place a bet before the day begins:

1. Check there are at least 2 meetings running in the day as you will need at least a minimum of 2 meetings to get to the minimum number of bets for a sequence within races 1-4. If there are at least 2 meetings proceed to step 2. If Not then there is no betting today and you can take a day off.

2. Check which races will be your qualifying races for your sequence. This is either 5,6 or 7 races. Make sure all of these races occur in the first 4 races of each meeting. If they do not then you can take a day off otherwise progress to step 3.

3. Ensure that no more than 3 qualifying races are not at the same track for a 5 or 6 race sequence. Ensure it is less then 4 qualifying races for a 7 race sequence. If it is more then this then you are done for the day and do not bet. Otherwise move to Step 4.

4. Check the pre post or fixed odds for the races. Check to see if they fit within your risk limit (10 units for 5 races, 15 units for 6 races and 25 units for 7 races). You can work this out by assuming each race is a losing race and performing the calculation through to the end. Your final loss figure needs to be less than the acceptable risk level. If it is close and you think the odds may drop then you may take a chance on the races. If it is substantially over (1 unit or more) then you get a day off. If the odds allow an acceptable risk level then move to Step 5.

5. Determine the approximate time you have between each race finishing and the next race starting. Make sure you are available for the whole time needed to place the bets for a complete losing run. Bots can be programmed to do this but if you decide to use a bot ensure there is adequate time to get the result before the next race starts.

6. One Minute before the race starts look at the odds and determine your bet size. (This is determined by (Profit Target + current Loss)/(odds-1). Place your bet at fixed odds (Betfair is a good choice).

7. If the horse wins you are finished for the day with a profit. If not then wait for your second qualifying race and go back to Step 6.

WHY YOU CAN LOSE FOLLOWING THIS SYSTEM

Why would I spend the entire book writing about how great this system is and then have a whole chapter dedicated to why it won't work? Its fairly simple really in that the reason it might not work for you is because of your psychology. The main reasons people stop using this system are:

- It is too boring
- You will deviate from the rules
- You will lose your nerve

These are the 3 most common reasons that will cause this system to fail. Notice that none of them are based on the system rules.

People find this system boring because as it has so little action throughout the day. If you win on your first bet then you are done for the day and can move onto something else. But people will want to start it again and bet on the second race like it was the first race. **DO NOT DO THIS**. This is a day by day system and you need to follow the rules as they are written. You stop at a winner for the day.

People will deviate from the rules and include too much risk by going one more bet or by increasing the amount they risk on a day by including very short odds on selections. The rules are there for a reason and have been thought out to provide the optimum solution. Deviating from the rules will only cause heartache when the big loss does come along.

People will commonly lose their nerve betting when it comes to the 4th or 5th bets and they haven't hit a winner. This might happen for 2 days in a row and so they say the system is useless and go try something else. Those 2 days might be followed by 20 profitable days.

The randomness of results in horse racing makes it very hard to predict which days will be the losing days. But the law of averages lets us know that eventually those profitable days will come along to make up for the losing days. You need to commit to this system for at least a month to see the results.

PAPER TRADING IS A REQUIREMENT

You should always paper trade a selection system for a period of time before taking the plunge with real money. I encourage you to do this to ensure you get all the calculations right and you understand the rules properly. Paper Trading the system will also give you the results and confidence to feel secure on using this with actual money.

Once you are confident in the system after paper trading you can move to small stakes. I suggest aiming for a very low profit target each day to ensure you get use to the feelings of betting with real money. It is very different to paper trading as you now have something to lose. Get comfortable with small stakes and then increase your stakes as your bank grows.

I always suggest starting with small bank ($300 or less) and only increase the staking when the bank increases. This way if the system does ever fail you in the future you are only out that initial $300.

PATIENCE – USE A DIFFERENT BANK FOR ACTION BETS

Patience is the key to this system.

You cannot be greedy or try and do this more than once a day. You need to be patient and gain the profits over time. Patient is a virtue and many punters do not have it. It you feel you need to have more action and more bets then set yourself up an action bank where you can take whatever bets you want to.

Do not compare or include these action bets with this system though as its apples and oranges. This system is a slow long term profitable solution compared to any "bets you just had to have" which will likely lose over the long term.

POSSIBLE PROBLEMS YOU COULD FACE FOLLOWING THIS SYSTEM

There are a few problems you may face when you start following this system that can arise from time to time.

The main things you may face are:
- You missed the first race or few races.
- There is a delay in a meeting.
- Joint Favourites

If you miss the first race or the first couple of races the first thing you need to do is check whether a winner would have been struck. If so then do not start betting. You have missed your chance for the day. If a winner has not been hit you can start your sequence of bets from the next race. Ensure that you still fit within all the rules of the system (for example Races 1-4 only at a meeting).

Delays at meetings occur for many things such as a fallen jockey or a horse which has raced off uncontrollably. If this occurs you should just move onto the next qualifying race. It can be too hard otherwise to track which races to include and exclude. This occurrence will not happen often enough to cause any major issues and will be very infrequent.

Joint favourites happen from time to time. This is where two horses are very close in price and you are not sure which one will be the favourite. In this case I suggest sticking with the pre post favourite. If they also happen to have the same pre post price then check a few bookies to get an idea on which one they have lowest. If this fails take the horse which is has the best last start figure. These are just a few suggestions to keep it simple. The other option you can take in some situation is to dutch the selections. This is where you bet on both selections to win. To do this both favourites need to be at a price at or higher than $4.00. This ensures that you will get back combined odds of at least $2.00 after the dutch bet. Personally though I would pick a favourite and live with the decision or just move onto the next race.

A FEW IMPORVEMENTS YOU MAY LIKE TO TRY

These improvements will increase your profit on turnover but will decrease the number of days you can bet. These improvements include:

- Exclude days/meetings where carnivals that are full of group races
- Exclude days when the weather is terrible

As stated earlier in the book the system makes it profits by targeting races where there are just a few horses could win. Generally group races are not races which you would want to be betting on. This is because all of the horses in the race have the ability to win. Compare to this to maidens and lower class races where a lot of the horses may never win a race in their lifetimes. For this reason you should avoid major carnivals and major race days where the majority of races are group races at a meeting.

Horses handle wet tracks very differently. Some horses can handle wet tracks much better then others. Wet tracks can sometimes cause some issues for the fancied horses unless they already have wet track form. For this reason favourites have a much lower strike rate on tracks which are rated DEAD or worse (SOFT or HEAVY). For this reason you should stick to tracks only rated as GOOD. I like to exclude all tracks which have a track rating below GOOD. This does mean that there are a lot of days in winter and spring when the tracks will be too wet to have a bet.

A SUGGESTION FOR YOUR SANITY

I encourage everyone to be confident in this system before you start betting on it. The best way to do this is to back test your selections.

In Australia you cancan use the Betfair Advantage Tool. This will show you the races in time order and you will be able to run through the rules very quickly for each day. I would recommend you do this for at least a month's worth of data which shouldn't take you longer then 30-45 mins.

For UK and Ireland I suggest using the At the Races website for results. Unfortunately you will not get these in time order like the Betfair Advantage Tool. You will need to manually work out which races come after each other.

For the US I recommend using the RacingPost website. As with the UK and Ireland form, you will need to manually work out the race order. You can also use AtTheRaces website as it does contain the US Racing as well.

By completing a run through historical data you will be able to see how the system works and make sure you are up to speed on the calculations for bet size.

FINAL THOUGHTS

This system is simple.

Almost too simple which will cause many punters to dismiss it. Other punters will dismiss it because of its Stop at a winner and yet other punters will dismiss it because it uses a martingale staking plan (all be it with safety mechanisms).

From 100 punters who read this I think only 3-5 will actually back test it. These 3-5 punters will actually go on to use it and make a long term profit. All the others will find reasons to condemn it before they actually go and test it.

If there is thought I can leave you with that you should take out of this book is that punters are set in their ways and believe old advice which may no longer be relevant. Challenge everything, including what it is written in this book, and either prove to yourself it works or prove it doesn't work.

Don't commit to a standpoint until you have tested and seen the results.

ABOUT THE AUTHOR

I am a long time punter who has investigated a lot of systems and ideas around horse racing. I spent countless hours devising complex equations and ratings and selection techniques in order to find the winner and beat my fellow punters. In the end I found what is simple usually works.

CPSIA information can be obtained at www.ICGtesting.com
Printed in the USA
LVOW05s2047040114

368094LV00023B/2089/P

9 781490 940939